Contents

Meet the families

The start of the 2000s was not that long ago, but an amazing amount has changed since then. During the decade the Internet continued to grow and affect our lives. Smartphones and social networking sites were invented. There were also new trends in fashion, music and television. Four children's families share their memories of those days.

Alice

Alice's family

Alice Hibberd is 13 years old and lives with her mother, Julie, and stepfather, Tony. Alice has an older sister called Meg, who was born in 1987 and was aged between 13 and 22 in the 2000s.

Meg

Sarah

Sarah's family

Sarah Hadland is 12 years old and lives with her brother, Jacob, and parents, Marcia and Dan. Jacob was 6 years old at the start of the decade and became a teenager in 2007. Sarah also has a half brother called James, who was born in 1986.

Dan

Jacob

James

MY FAMILY REMEMBERS

The 2000s

James Nixon

W
FRANKLIN WATTS

Franklin Watts
This edition published in Great Britain in 2015
by The Watts Publishing Group

Planned and produced by Discovery Books Ltd., 2 College Street,
Ludlow, Shropshire, SY8 1AN
www.discoverybooks.net
Editor: James Nixon
Design: Blink Media

Photo credits: Apple Inc: p. 11 middle, Bigstock: p. 23 top; Bobby Humphrey: pp. 8 top, 9 top, 12 top, 13 middle-left, 15 left, 17 middle, 19 bottom, 24 top and left, 25; BSkyB Ltd.: 9 middle; Chris Fairclough: pp. 10 top and middle, 11 top, 13 top and right, 23 bottom-right; Shutterstock: pp. 6 bottom (Adrin Shamsudin), 7 top (Darko Zeljkovic), 7 bottom (1000 Words), 11 top-left (Zakharoff), 11 bottom (Monkey Business Images), 20 left and bottom, 23 middle, 27 top (Ashley Pickering), 27 middle (Pincasso); Getty Images: pp. 8 left (Lakruwan Wanniarachchi); Photoshot: pp. 10 bottom (Imagebrokers), 16 middle (Sebastian Widmann/Picture Alliance), 17 bottom (Achim Scheidemann/Picture Alliance); Rex Features: pp. 14 (Mark St George), 15 top (Ken McKay), 18 (20thC.Fox/Everett), 19 top (W. Disney/Everett), 21 top (ITV), 21 bottom, 22 (Ray Tang); Visit Britain: p. 29 bottom (Southend-on-Sea Bor. Council); Wikimedia: pp. 6 top (TheMachineStops/upstateNYer), 16 top (Evan-Amos), 20 top, 26 top and bottom, 27 bottom, 28 top (Tom Collins), 29 top (Robert Kalina), 29 middle, 30 (David Rydevik).
Cover photos: Shutterstock: left (haveseen), right (Edyta Pawlowska).
Every attempt has been made to clear copyright. Should there be any inadvertent omission please apply to the publisher for rectification.

Dewey number: 941

ISBN: 978 1 4451 4358 3

Printed in China

Franklin Watts
An imprint of
Hachette Children's Group
Part of The Watts Publishing Group
Carmelite House
50 Victoria Embankment
London EC4Y 0DZ

An Hachette UK Company
www.hachette.co.uk

www.franklinwatts.co.uk

MIX
Paper from
responsible sources
FSC® C104740
FSC
www.fsc.org

Words that are **bold** in the text are explained in the glossary.

Matty

Hazel

Matty's family

Matty Morris is 12 years old. He lives with his younger sister, Milly, his older brother, Peter, and his parents, Julie and Kevin. Peter was aged between 3 and 12 in the 2000s.

Hazel's family

Hazel Stancliffe is 11 years old. She lives with her older sister, Lily, and her parents, Abigail and Paul. Lily was born in 1997 and was a young child growing up in the 2000s.

Julie

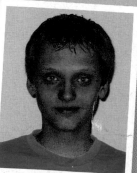

Peter

Abigail

Lily

The noughties

The 'noughties' is a nickname sometimes given to the 2000s. It was a time when there were many exciting changes in technology. But, there was also a darker side to the decade as fears of **terrorism** grew across the world.

On September 11, 2001 (9/11), terrorists **hijacked** four US passenger planes and flew two of them into the Twin Tower skyscrapers in New York, and one into the Pentagon in Washington DC. In total, nearly 3,000 people were killed. Four years later, bombs were set off in London killing 56 people.

The Twin Towers in New York went up in flames in 2001 when two planes were crashed into them. Within two hours both buildings had collapsed killing 2,606 people.

Sarah asks her dad about life in the 2000s: There was lots of fear around after the 9/11 terrorist attacks. In Birmingham we started seeing a lot more armed police on the streets and **CCTV** cameras started appearing everywhere. It made me feel a bit worried when I was travelling on a bus or train.

CCTV camera

'There was lots of fear around.'

As the Internet grew, people spent more and more time in front of a computer screen. An increasing number of people were going online to shop and talk to their friends. Wireless technology improved in the mid-2000s, which meant it was easy to connect to the Internet on your laptop or mobile phone as you travelled.

Mobile phones and laptop devices could connect to the Internet using radio signals instead of wires.

Social networking sites, where you could chat and share photos, were a great way to keep in touch with people even if they were thousands of kilometres away. It was the biggest change in the way that people communicated with each other since the invention of the telephone.

The Myspace social networking site was launched in 2003 and Facebook (left) began in 2004.

Hazel asks her sister what was new in the 2000s:

I remember when everyone started getting into social networking. If you didn't join in with it you felt left out at school because everybody would be telling each other about things online.

TIME DIFFERENCE

The number of Facebook users grew from 5 million in late 2005 to nearly 400 million by the end of the decade!

Technology at home

The number of households in Britain that had the Internet rose from 20 per cent in 2000 to 73 per cent by the end of the decade.

Broadband Internet was developed which could carry much more information on telephone lines. It made the Internet work a lot quicker and helped to make the Web much more popular. By 2010, over 30 million adults in the UK used the Internet every day.

With broadband, a filter separates the voice and Internet signals on your telephone line. This made the Web work much faster.

The Internet began to take over from newspapers and books as the main way to get news and information.

'It made a screeching noise and took for ever.'

Alice asks her sister about the early Internet: Before broadband came in you had to 'dial up' with the same line as your telephone to log on to the Internet. It made a screeching noise and took for ever. My parents used to get mad at me for being on the Internet too long because they could not use the telephone at the same time.

Digital cameras quickly became very popular in the 2000s as they got better and cheaper. Like many gadgets they also got smaller and smaller as time went on.

CAMEDIA
OLYMPUS
C-220 ZOOM
OLYMPUS LENS

A digital camera from 2002.

Alice's sister, Meg, as a teenager in the 2000s.

At the start of the 2000s, televisions in the home were very different from today. Most homes had a bulky TV with a **cathode ray tube** inside, instead of a flat panel TV. The picture through a TV aerial could be very fuzzy because the signal was not digital. By the end of the decade most homes had a digital set-top box. Some of these boxes let you pause and rewind live television programmes.

Matty's family watch their television in the 2000s.

At the end of the 2000s, set-top boxes like this one offered television in **high definition**.

DVD players replaced video recorders in most homes. Blu-ray discs were developed in 2006 that could store video in high definition. They were named after the blue laser used to read the disc.

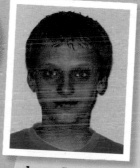

Matty asks his brother how he watched TV:
I remember when the man came in a van to deliver our Sky + set-top box. It was brilliant – it made watching TV so much more fun. If you liked a bit you could rewind it and slow it right down.

Hazel asks her sister about changes in technology:
I was really upset when videos ended and they said no more would be made. We had built up such a big collection of videos and our video player still worked.

At work

In the 2000s, most people in Britain worked in service industries. Service industries sell goods or provide a service. Jobs in this industry include shop workers, dentists, teachers and travel agents. Only 13 per cent of people worked in manufacturing (the making of goods).

Many **migrants** came to the UK to find work. They often did low-paid jobs, such as cleaning and labouring, that British people did not want to do. Between 2004 and 2009, 1.5 million workers came from countries which had just joined the **European Union**, such as Poland and the Czech Republic.

There were lots of jobs in service industries in the 2000s, such as hairdressing (left) or bike repairs (below).

Polish workers pick crops on a farm in the UK in 2005.

Hazel asks her mum what work she did:

In 2006, I started work with a group of migrant workers from places like Poland. I had to help their language skills so they could give information and help to other migrants. I was so impressed with how quickly they could pick up the English language and learn new skills.

Technology continued to improve in the workplace in the 2000s. Flash drives took over from floppy disks as a way of storing computer files. They were smaller, faster and could store much more information. Email became the standard way to write and send documents.

Flash drive

Email and the Internet made communicating much easier for office workers in the 2000s.

Smartphones such as the Blackberry began to take off at the start of the decade. These pocket computers had wireless email and were very handy for workers on the move. Smartphones became so powerful that they were soon in high demand with everyone. Phones became cameras, MP3 players and web browsers all in one, with the ability to download many more applications.

The iPhone smartphone with its touchscreen first came out in 2007 and was a huge success.

TIME DIFFERENCE

In 2000, there were 35 million mobile phones in use. In 2010, there were nearly 75 million.

Matty asks his brother about mobile phones: About 2005 I got my first mobile phone. It was really small and the screen slid up to reveal the keypad. I thought it was really cool because none of my friends had one.

Going shopping

In the 2000s, more and more people started shopping for goods on their computer. Most high street shops had a website you could order from. You could even order your food shopping online, and have it delivered to your door.

In fact, almost every kind of service became available on the Internet. You could book holidays, buy train tickets, pay bills and manage your bank account all online.

ebay®

Ebay was a big success in the 2000s. It gave everyone the chance to buy and sell goods online. Here is its logo.

TIME DIFFERENCE

British households spent 6 billion pounds in total over the Internet in 2002. By the end of the decade, the amount spent online had risen to nearly 40 billion pounds.

Sarah asks her half brother about online shopping:
Ebay was one of the first sites I used on the Internet. I used to go on there with my dad and he helped me find parts for my computer and bits for my Playstation. It was a great way of finding rare things as cheaply as possible.

Town centres had to compete with out-of-town superstores and websites. It was often only the big **chain stores** which could afford to stay in business. This meant towns across the country looked very similar with the same shops.

Most big towns had the same shops on their high streets.

Retail parks on the edge of town continued to be popular in the 2000s, and took business away from town centres.

To attract customers, shops would often have discount sales nearly all year round and not just in January (right).

People were more aware of the environment in the 2000s. Many decided to stop using plastic carrier bags, which were thrown away and could not be recycled. Instead they used a reusable bag such as this one (left).

Matty asks his mum how she shopped:
In the early 2000s, I set up an account on the Next website so I could order clothes online. It changed my shopping habits for ever. It seemed so much easier than going into town.

'It seemed so much easier than going into town.'

3

Entertainment

In the 2000s, there were more forms of entertainment in the home than ever before. Video games, the Internet and social networking grew in popularity. However, television continued to be a major source of enjoyment.

TV in the decade will be mostly remembered for the rise of **reality TV**. *Big Brother* started in 2000 and ran for ten years. In the show, viewers watched a group of ordinary people in a house full of cameras, and voted one person out each week. It was a big hit and sparked many similar programmes.

In *Big Brother*, you could watch the housemates all day. Reality TV made the contestants very famous for a short time, while some became big celebrities.

'I couldn't understand why I found it so addictive.'

Sarah asks her brother about his favourite reality TV:

We used to love watching *Big Brother*. I would watch it live even if all of the housemates were in bed sleeping. I couldn't really understand why I found it so addictive.

Another kind of reality TV show that took off was the talent competition. *Pop Idol* (2001) was a sensation and made the first ever winner Will Young a star. Pop Idol was replaced by *The X Factor* (2004) and there were other shows with a panel of judges such as *Fame Academy* (2002) and *Britain's Got Talent* (2007).

Many reality shows featured celebrities, such as *Strictly Come Dancing*, and *I'm a Celebrity Get Me Out of Here!* set in the Australian rainforest.

Fantasy was popular in the noughties. In 2005, *Doctor Who* returned to the TV screens after a fifteen-year break and gained many new, young fans. The *Harry Potter* novels written by JK Rowling were successful across the world and were popular with adults as well as children.

Many reality shows featured celebrities. *Dancing on Ice* was a celebrity skating competition in front of a panel of judges.

Doctor Who toys were popular because of the TV show.

Alice asks her sister about the books she read:

My favourite *Harry Potter* was *The Goblet of Fire*. He had to battle past dragons, sea creatures and a terrible maze. One of the best bits was when he ate a weird, slimy plant that turned him into a fish, so he could swim underwater and rescue his friends from beneath a lake.

Video gaming

By the end of the 2000s, the video games industry had become bigger than the film or music business. Games continued to look ever more stunning and realistic.

The Playstation 2, launched in 2000, became the best-selling console of all time. In 2006, it was replaced by the Playstation 3. Microsoft's Xbox (2001) and the follow-up, the Xbox 360 (2005), were also very popular.

The Xbox was released in 2001.

The newest consoles, such as this Playstation 3, featured high-definition graphics and had wireless game controllers.

Sarah asks her half brother how he played video games: By the time of the Playstation 3, graphics were much better. Around a dozen of my friends would squash into a little bedroom to play games. If you lost it was bad news – you had to pass the controller to the next person and it was ages before you got another turn.

The Sims was a hugely successful series of games on the PC in the early 2000s. It was very popular with girls and people who were not into other types of video games.

The Sims 'simulated' real life and you could buy a house, arrange parties and go on dates.

Guitar Hero (right) was a surprise hit in 2005. You had to press buttons in time with the music. It sparked a wave of 'rhythm games'.

Matty asks his brother what games he had:

I had a rhythm game called *Donkey Konga* on my Nintendo Game Cube. It came with drums and you had to keep to the beat of the music. You could speed it up and make it mega hard. I was amazing at the game and I always beat my friends and my dad.

Matty's brother, Peter, playing on his Xbox in his bedroom.

Nintendo released two products which made gaming very different. The handheld Nintendo DS used a touchscreen while the Nintendo Wii was controlled by the way you moved. Its games, such as *Wii Sports*, were enjoyed by the whole family.

Hazel asks her sister about her memories of games consoles:

In 2007, my class at school bought a Nintendo Wii. If we earned enough points for doing good work we got to play on it at the end of the week.

Two girls play the *Wii Sports* boxing game. To punch the opponent you had to swing the controllers back and forth.

On film

Going to the cinema remained a popular pastime in the 2000s. Films were made to look more spectacular as **computer generated imagery (CGI)** and 3D technology advanced.

Avatar was the biggest blockbuster of the decade. It cost around 300 million dollars to make.

'It felt like you were in the film'

The amazing effects of CGI could be seen in *Shrek* (2001), *King Kong* (2005) and then the science fiction blockbuster *Avatar* in 2009. This film set on the alien moon of Pandora made over 2 billion dollars worldwide. It could be watched in 3D and became a must-see event.

Matty asks his brother if he saw *Avatar*:
I went to watch *Avatar* at the cinema on a school trip. The 3D was amazing. It felt like you were in the film, especially when the wings of the alien dragon were flapping around right in front of your face.

Computers could create special effects that had not been possible in the past. Battle scenes in films such as *Gladiator* (2000) and *The Lord of the Rings* **trilogy** were incredible.

Sequels were a great way for film-makers to make money. *The Pirates of the Caribbean* and *Star Wars* films were big favourites and the *Harry Potter* books were brought to life at the cinema with huge success.

Johnny Depp as Captain Jack Sparrow (right) stars in *Pirates of the Caribbean: Dead Man's Chest* (2006), the second film in the series.

Hazel asks her sister what films she liked:
I went to see *Harry Potter and the Philosopher's Stone* with my dad at the big cinema in Leicester Square in London. The special effects were so real it was scary. After that I was hooked on Harry Potter and I wanted to read all of the books.

Some types of film became popular once again in the 2000s. There were comic book heroes, such as *Spiderman* (2002) and dazzling musicals, such as *Moulin Rouge* (2001). Animations such as *Monsters Inc* (2001), *Finding Nemo* (2003) and *Cars* (2006) were enjoyed by children.

A *Cars* jigsaw puzzle based on the film.

From CDs to iPods

There were big changes in the way people listened to music in the 2000s. Music data could be stored on small MP3 files. Instead of buying CDs, people began buying tunes over the Internet by downloading them to their computer.

MP3 players were much smaller than CD players and easier to carry around. The fashionable range of iPods started in 2001 and it was one of the biggest selling gadgets of the decade.

The iPod Classic in 2005 (top) and the tiny iPod Shuffle.

Alice asks her sister how she listened to music:

I listened to CDs on my black stereo player that could hold five CDs at once. I also had a CD Walkman, which I always took with me in the back of the car on long journeys. The album I listened to more than any other was the *Marshall Mathers LP* by Eminem.

Some people still bought CDs because they liked the product, which came with artwork and lyrics to the songs. However, many CD shops had to close down. Musicians made less money as people shared and downloaded music files, both legally and **illegally**.

Portable CD player

In the charts, pop music aimed at young teenagers continued to do well. Girl groups such as Girls Aloud were popular. Many of the successful acts had made their names on TV talent competitions, such as *The X Factor* winner Leona Lewis.

2006 *X Factor* winner Leona Lewis became an international star.

TIME DIFFERENCE

Sales of CD singles dropped from 55 million in 2000 to 2.5 million in 2009.

Usher performing the number one hit single *Yeah* in 2004.

Electronic sounds made a comeback in the 2000s in pop and rock music. **R'n'B** was another popular style of music and Beyonce was a big star. The best-selling artist of the decade was rapper *Eminem*.

Sarah asks her brother about the music he liked:
I listened to R'n'B artists mainly, such as Usher and Ne-Yo. My favourite album was *Raymond vs Raymond* by Usher and I used to sing the songs off it on our karaoke machine at home.

In fashion

In the 2000s, clothes were a mixture of styles from previous decades. In general, fashions were less casual and minimal than they had been in the 1990s.

Clothes tended to be more narrow and tighter fitting for both men and women. Denim remained popular. At the start of the decade it had to be dark denim. Later on, skinny jeans were in fashion.

As the decade went on, clothes for women had a much more feminine look. Dresses, skirts and very high heels became everyday wear. The Boho style featured flowing tops and dresses, usually in bright patterns.

Celebrities had an influence on the clothes we wore in the 2000s. Some, such as Kate Moss, created their own lines to be sold in the high street shops.

'Everybody wore skinny jeans but I hated them.'

Hazel asks her sister about fashion in the 2000s:

Everybody wore skinny jeans but I hated them because they were so uncomfortable. My friends were obsessive in following the fashion trends and so was my sister, Hazel. She would cake her face in make-up and wear high heels.

Hip hop fashions were very popular. Followers of this trend wore hoodies, sweatpants and sometimes lots of '**bling**'.

A hoodie was a popular piece of urban clothing for young men in the 2000s.

In 2006, a more casual fashion trend took hold. It was called the Ugg boot (right). Another trend was for women to wear fake accessories to make them look glamorous. This included hair extensions, spray tans and false eyelashes!

Ugg boot

Alice's sister, Meg (left), and a friend dressed up for a party in the late 2000s.

Sarah asks her brother about hairstyles:
I had an afro hairstyle in the 2000s (below, far right). I used to comb my hair for hours with an **afro pick** to make it perfectly round. I was always late for school, but when I got there everybody wanted to touch it.

Schooldays

A teaching assistant helps children in their maths lesson.

In the 2000s, lots of money was spent on schools to make them better. New schools were built to replace old crumbling buildings. There were new pieces of equipment for lessons and break time, and more teaching assistants to help teachers do their job.

Different types of school were set up to give parents the choice where they sent their children. Many schools specialised in a particular subject or area. Other schools became **academies**, which meant they were free to teach differently from other schools.

Hazel asks her sister about the school she went to:
My school was an academy and was very strict. I remember losing my tie and I was terrified about going to school. In the end my mum had to drive me into town to buy a new one.

Hazel (left) and her sister, Lily, in a school photo in 2006.

Interactive whiteboards with teacher presentations, games and activities replaced blackboards.

Technology was having a bigger impact in the classroom. Pupils could do their research on the Internet as well as the school library.

In 2005, the celebrity chef Jamie Oliver worked with schools to make school dinners healthier. Junk foods, such as chips and Turkey Twizzlers were taken off lunch menus across the country.

A school dinner menu from 2007.

Class Catering   HEART SMART   Menu 07   CLASS catering

	MONDAY	TUESDAY	WEDNESDAY	THURSDAY	FRIDAY
Week 1	Sausages & Yorkshire Puds with Boiled Potatoes & Gravy	Beef Lasagne with Garlic Bread	Chicken Korma with Brown Rice	Roast Pork & Apple Sauce with Creamed & Roast Potatoes	Tuna Pasta Bake
	Roasted Vegetable Wraps with Crusty Bread	Pasta Provencal with Garlic Bread	Cauliflower & Broccoli		Quorn Burger in a Bap with Chips
		Coleslaw & Sliced Carrots	Cheese with Herby Diced Potatoes	Leek & Mushroom Bake with Creamed & Roast Potatoes	
	Mixed Salad & Broccoli		Sweet corn & Carrots		Peas & Baked Beans
		Rhubarb Squares with Fresh Milk		Cauliflower & Swede	
	Treacle Sponge & Custard		Chocolate & Mandarin Muffin		Neapolitan Sponge & Custard
				Apple & Cherry Crumble & Ice Cream	
Week 2	Beef Bolognaise with Pasta Quills	Fish Cake with Parsley Potatoes	Roast Turkey with Creamed & Roast Potatoes	Beef & Vegetable Pie with New Potatoes	Chicken Fajitas
	Quorn & Vegetable Lasagne with Garlic bread	Pasta with Tomato & Basil Sauce	Savoury Vegetable Slice with Creamed & Roast Potatoes	Mediterranean Vegetable Risotto with Crusty Bread	Vegetable Stir Fry with Noodles
	Broccoli & Mixed Salad	Baked Beans & Green Beans		Sweet corn & Peas	Mixed Salad & Mini Corn on the Cob
		Jam & Coconut Sponge	Carrots & Green Cabbage	Cucumber Sticks & Grated Carrots	
	Chocolate & Pear Delight		Fresh Fruit Salad & Shortbread Biscuits	Oaty Apple Pie & Custard	Carrot Cake with Vanilla Icing
Week 3	Oven Baked Burger with Sauté Potatoes	Roast Chicken & Stuffing with Creamed & Roast Potatoes	Turkey & Spinach Balti with Boiled Rice	Lamb Shepherds Pie with Boiled Potatoes	Salmon Tagliatelle
	Cheese & Red Onion Quiche	Cheesy Omelette with Creamed & Roast Potatoes	Cheese & Potato Bake with Crusty Bread	Vegetable Chilli with Boiled Rice	Cheese & Tomato Pizza with New Potatoes
	Coleslaw & Tomato Salad & Baked Beans	Green Beans & Cauliflower	Cucumber Riatta & Plum Tomatoes	Peas & Carrots	Green Salad & Sweet corn
	Sticky Toffee Pudding & Chocolate Sauce	Apple Flapjack with Fruit Juice Drink	Apricot & Date Shortbread with Vanilla Sauce	Lemon Drizzle Cake	Iced Fruit Bun

Fresh cold drinking water will be available daily
A further selection of drinks to include—Water, Juice, Milk, Milkshakes & Smoothies will be available to purchase at middle schools only or as required.

A selection of breads & variety of salads will be available each day.
A choice of Jacket Potatoes with a selection of fillings will be available daily as an alternative option where required.

Pupils were encouraged to eat healthy foods, such as salads and vegetables, at lunchtime.

Sarah asks her brother about his memories of school:

My biggest memory at school was when a **meteorite** landed on the school field while we were playing on it. The sky looked weird and then there was a loud boom as it landed. The meteorite was the size of a cannonball. Soon there were cameramen on the scene taking pictures of it for the newspapers.

Travelling

Toyota Prius

Global warming was a big worry for the world in the 2000s. Scientists thought that pollution from vehicles was one of the main causes. This led to cleaner modes of transport being developed.

Hybrid vehicles combined a petrol engine with electric motors, and released less **carbon dioxide** into the air. Hybrid cars, such as the Toyota Prius and Honda Insight, were popular in the mid-2000s. Some environmentally friendly vehicles used different fuels, such as **biofuel**.

'It used to bother me that we were polluting the air.'

Alice asks her sister how she used to travel:
I wish our family could have had a hybrid car but they were too expensive. It used to really bother me that we were polluting the air too much. For each trip I made, I used to work out if I had time to walk instead.

A tram operates on the new tramway system which was built in South London in 2000.

To reduce pollution in London a **'congestion** charge' had to be paid by people driving into the city centre. In some cities tramlines were built. Petrol was not just dirty – it was also getting very expensive. In 2001, there were fuel protests at the rising cost of fuel.

Speed cameras were placed on many roads to stop drivers going too fast. A gadget which arrived in the 2000s was the satellite navigation (sat nav) system that many people use today. They directed the driver to their destination, but also warned you of speed cameras ahead.

Speed camera

In 2008, more than three million sat nav systems were sold in the UK.

Matty asks his brother when they got a sat nav:
We got a sat nav in about 2004. Dad used to get really annoyed with the voice. When she said 'please turn right' she didn't pronounce the 't' properly at the end.

The massive Airbus A380 is put on display in 2005 shortly before its first flight.

There was a big increase in the number of plane journeys people were taking. In 2007, the Airbus A380 was built. Seating up to 850 people it was the largest passenger plane in the world!

Holidays

Travelling by plane was very affordable in the 2000s.

By the end of the 2000s, the number of holiday trips people took to other countries had increased to nearly 70 million! In comparison, there were less than 20 million trips abroad in the mid-'80s.

Plane tickets got much cheaper. Low-cost airlines such as EasyJet and RyanAir provided a basic service. They were more affordable, but if you wanted a meal or drinks you had to pay extra.

France and Spain remained the most popular holiday destinations, but people were trying more **exotic** parts of the world, too. Places in South-east Asia, such as Thailand, attracted many visitors. More and more holidaymakers were taking short breaks as an extra holiday in European cities, such as Prague or Rome.

Sarah asks her brother about the holidays he went on: We went to Jamaica twice in the 2000s. I remember climbing this amazing waterfall that fell into the sea, called Dunn's River. I slipped and nearly fell off the cliff edge but luckily an American man standing behind me caught and saved me!

Sarah stands next to her brother, Jacob, while on a family holiday to Lanzarote (left) and Jacob paddles down a river in Jamaica (right).

Matty asks his brother about his holiday memories:
Most summers we went abroad. In 2004, we went to Kefalonia in Greece, with family and friends. Matty jumped in our hotel swimming pool with his arms up in the air and his armbands shot off. Uncle Steve had to dive in and save him from the bottom of the pool. I have never laughed so much.

On 1 January 2002, 16 European countries changed their notes and coins to the Euro currency. Now it was easier to travel between these countries because you didn't need to change the money you were carrying. The UK did not join the Euro and decided to keep pounds and pence.

A 100 Euro note and coins.

More families took their summer holiday in the UK in the late 2000s. It was cheaper than going abroad and people saw that there were wonderful places to visit close to home.

British resorts and national parks had to work hard to encourage people to holiday in the UK. Towards the end of the decade the **'staycation'** became more popular once again.

Find out what your family remembers

Try asking members of your family what they remember about the 2000s. You could ask them the same questions that children in this book have asked and then compare the answers you get. Ask your relatives how they think that life in the 2000s was different from today. Get them to talk about their favourite memories or important events of the time. This will help you build up your own picture of life in the 2000s. It will also help you find out more about your family history.

A tsunami strikes Thailand in 2004.

Timeline

2000 The first series of reality show *Big Brother* is screened.

2001 Foot and Mouth disease hits farm animals across the country.
The Microsoft Xbox is launched.
The first iPod is developed and sold in shops.
The 9/11 terrorist attacks in the USA kill nearly 3,000 people.
The war in Afghanistan begins in response to the 9/11 attacks.

2002 On 1 January, 16 European countries adopt the Euro currency.
Will Young beats rival Gareth Gates to become the first winner of *Pop Idol*.

2003 The USA and the UK invade Iraq.

2004 The social networking site Facebook is launched.
On Boxing Day, an earthquake under the Indian Ocean triggers a **tsunami** that kills over 230,000 people in 14 countries.

2005 Terrorists bomb London's transport system on the 7 July.

2006 The Nintendo Wii is released.
Sky starts showing television in high definition.

2007 Smoking is banned in public places across the UK.
The first iPhone smartphone goes on sale.

2009 *Avatar* premieres in cinemas and can be viewed in 3D.

Glossary

academy
A school which is free to run itself and teach differently from other schools.

afro pick
A comb with wide and loose teeth, used to make an afro hairstyle big and round.

biofuel
A fuel made from living things such as plants.

bling
Flashy jewellery.

broadband
A system which sends Internet signals down a telephone line without blocking voice signals.

carbon dioxide
A gas that humans breathe out and is produced by burning fossil fuels.

cathode ray tube
A wide tube in which an electric charge is beamed on to a fluorescent screen to form images. They were used in old televisions and computer monitors.

CCTV
A system in which video is recorded by fixed cameras. CCTV stands for closed-circuit television.

chain store
A shop that is found in many different towns and are all owned by the same company.

computer generated imagery (CGI)
Visual effects in films created by computers.

congestion
A term used when the roads are full or overcrowded.

digital
The system of carrying information, such as sounds and images, that is used in computers.

European Union
A group of European countries set up to help each other and make trade easier between its members.

exotic
Describes places that are unusual and a long distance away.

global warming
The gradual increase in temperatures across the world caused by higher levels of carbon dioxide and other pollutants.

high definition
Describes images that are more detailed than those on traditional television sets.

hijack
To take control of a vehicle illegally.

hip hop
A style of pop music which contains rapping and electronic sounds.

illegal
Against the law.

meteorite
A piece of rocky material from space that has landed on Earth.

migrant
A person that moves from one country to another.

radio signals
Electrical waves sent through the air, used by mobile phones and other devices to carry messages.

reality TV
A show starring people being themselves, such as living together in a house or taking part in a talent competition.

R'n'B
Short for 'rhythm and blues'. A form of pop music with its origins in black American music.

sequel
A book or film which continues the story of a previous one.

staycation
A holiday in your own country.

terrorism
The use of extreme violence to try to bring about change.

trilogy
A series of three books or films that feature the same characters or subject.

tsunami
A series of enormous waves that destroys coastal areas.

Further information

Books

Home Life (Britain Since 1948), by Neil Tonge (Wayland), 2010
How Have Things Changed series, by James Nixon (Franklin Watts), 2008
Popular Culture (Britain Since 1948), by Stewart Ross (Wayland), 2010
Technology (Britain Since 1948), by Neil Champion (Wayland), 2010

Index